Maha Mrityunjaya Mantra

Awaken the Immortal Within
With Sacred Vibration Frequencies

Dr. Jilesh

Copyright © 2023 by Jilesh Thilakan

For permissions requests, write to the publisher at the address below:

Publisher: Jilesh Thilakan, India
Website: www.healingoraclewisdom.com
Email: drjilesht@gmail.com

Cover design by Jilesh Thilakan

Disclaimer: The information provided in this book is for general informational purposes only. The content is based on the Maha Mrityunjaya Mantra and its significance in various spiritual traditions. The author and publisher make no representation or warranty regarding the accuracy, efficacy, or outcomes resulting from the use of the Maha Mrityunjaya Mantra described in this book.

The reader understands and acknowledges that spiritual practices and experiences may vary. It is important to exercise personal discernment and respect individual beliefs and cultural traditions. The author and publisher disclaim any liability for any loss or damage incurred by the reader or any third party directly or indirectly as a result of the use or application of the information presented in this book.

The Maha Mrityunjaya Mantra is a sacred chant and should be approached with reverence and sincerity. If you have any specific concerns about its use or application, please consult with a qualified spiritual teacher or practitioner.

About the Author

Dr. Jilesh is a renowned and highly rated manifestation expert, spell caster, psychotherapist, life coach, and master of business administration. With extensive experience and expertise in the field, Dr. Jilesh has garnered a reputation as a trusted authority in the realm of manifestation and personal transformation.

As a highly rated manifestation expert and spell caster on Fiverr, Check Global Reviews here - https://www.fiverr.com/jileshthilakan?up_rollout=true Dr.Jilesh has assisted countless individuals in manifesting their desires and achieving their goals. Through his deep understanding of the principles of manifestation, Dr. Jilesh has helped clients tap into their innate power to create their dream reality.

In addition to his work on Fiverr, Dr. Jilesh has also excelled as a highly rated instructor on Udemy, with more than 30k students Check his personal development courses here - https://www.udemy.com/user/jilesh-thilakan/ sharing his knowledge and empowering students worldwide to harness the power of manifestation. With a passion for teaching and a commitment to providing valuable insights, Dr. Jilesh has garnered a loyal following of students who have experienced transformation and success under his guidance.

Dr. Jilesh's expertise extends beyond manifestation, as he is also a qualified psychotherapist and life coach. His background in psychology and counselling allows him to provide holistic support to individuals seeking personal growth and transformation. Through his empathetic approach and profound insights, Dr. Jilesh helps clients overcome challenges, break through limiting beliefs, and create lasting positive change in their lives.

Furthermore, Dr. Jilesh holds a master's degree in business administration, which adds a unique perspective to his work. His understanding of business principles and strategies allows him to guide individuals in aligning their personal goals with professional success, creating a harmonious balance between their aspirations and career pursuits.

With a diverse skill set and a genuine passion for helping others, Dr. Jilesh is committed to empowering individuals to unlock their full potential and manifest a life of abundance, fulfilment, and joy. Through his teachings, guidance, and transformative techniques, he aims to inspire and support others on their journey towards manifesting their deepest desires and living their best lives. For more about Author checkout his Blog- https://www.healingoraclewisdom.com/

Introduction

In the depths of our existence lies an extraordinary truth waiting to be unveiled-an immortal essence that transcends the limitations of our mortal selves. Within the ancient realm of spirituality, a profound tool awaits those who seek to awaken this immortal nature. Welcome to "Maha Mrityunjaya Mantra: Awaken the Immortal Within with Sacred Vibration Frequencies," a transformative journey into the realms of divine consciousness and eternal awakening.

This book is an exploration into the untapped reservoirs of our being, where the Maha Mrityunjaya Mantra resounds like a celestial melody, calling us to remember our divine heritage. Throughout the ages, this sacred mantra has echoed through the hearts of seekers, illuminating the path towards self-realization and the ultimate realization of immortality.

Within these pages, you will embark on a captivating voyage, guided by the power of sacred vibrations, as we delve deep into the mysteries of the Maha Mrityunjaya Mantra. Prepare to be captivated, inspired, and forever transformed as we unlock the secrets to living a life connected to the eternal realm.

What can you expect from this extraordinary journey? Brace yourself for an immersive exploration of the mantra's ancient origins and its profound significance in the tapestry of spiritual traditions. We will dive into the essence of each sacred word, unearthing the hidden gems of wisdom concealed within their syllables.

But this book is not just a theoretical exploration; it is a practical guide for experiencing the transformative effects of the Maha Mrityunjaya Mantra first-hand. Discover the proper techniques and sacred practices for chanting the mantra, as well as the profound benefits it bestows upon those who embrace its vibrations. From physical healing to expanded consciousness, the transformative power of this mantra knows no bounds.

As we journey deeper into the realms of spirituality, we will explore the science behind mantras and sound vibrations, bridging the ancient wisdom with modern understanding. Prepare to be astounded by scientific research and studies that validate the profound impact of sacred vibrations on our physical, mental, and spiritual well-being.

This book will not only enlighten your mind but also touch your heart. Through captivating stories and mystical experiences, you will witness the profound transformations that individuals have undergone through the power of the Maha Mrityunjaya Mantra. These accounts will inspire you, igniting the spark of curiosity within you and nurturing a yearning to explore the boundless realms of your own potential.

Moreover, we will delve into the symbiotic relationship between sacred symbols, yantras, and the Maha Mrityunjaya Mantra, amplifying the divine energies and expanding the boundaries of our spiritual connection. Learn how to create a sacred space and incorporate rituals and offerings to deepen your communion with the divine.

Prepare to be enveloped in a tapestry of ancient wisdom, scientific exploration, personal anecdotes, and practical techniques, all woven together to empower you to embrace the immortal essence that resides within your being. Through the Maha Mrityunjaya Mantra and sacred vibration frequencies, you will be guided on a transformative journey, enabling you to awaken the immortal within.

Are you ready to embark on this extraordinary odyssey? Open your heart, still your mind, and let the words on these pages resonate deep within your soul. It is time to awaken the immortal within. The divine symphony awaits.

Chapter 1
Introduction to the Maha Mrityunjaya Mantra

In the vast tapestry of ancient spiritual traditions, certain mantras have stood the test of time, resonating with profound wisdom and transformative power. Among these sacred incantations, the Maha Mrityunjaya Mantra holds a place of unparalleled significance. It is a mantra that beckons us to explore the depths of our being, awakening the immortal essence that lies dormant within.

Origins and Significance

The Maha Mrityunjaya Mantra traces its origins back to the ancient Hindu scriptures, the Rigveda. It is found in the sacred hymn known as the Rigveda Samhita (7.59.12). This timeless mantra has been revered by sages, yogis, and seekers for thousands of years, transcending cultural and geographical boundaries.

The word "Maha" denotes greatness, magnificence, and supreme power. "Mrityunjaya" translates to "conqueror of death" or "victory over death." Thus, the Maha Mrityunjaya Mantra is a divine invocation that calls upon the conqueror of death, urging us to embrace our inherent immortality.

The Power of Sacred Vibrations

At the heart of the Maha Mrityunjaya Mantra lies the concept of sacred vibrations. The ancients believed that everything in the universe, including our bodies and minds, is composed of vibrating energy. These vibrations create a subtle interplay between our inner and outer worlds, influencing our thoughts, emotions, and overall well-being.

When chanted with devotion and understanding, the Maha Mrityunjaya Mantra releases potent vibrations that reverberate through our entire being. It is said that these vibrations penetrate the depths of our consciousness, resonating with the divine frequencies that underpin the universe. By aligning ourselves with these sacred vibrations, we open ourselves to profound transformation and spiritual awakening.

The Call to Remember

The Maha Mrityunjaya Mantra serves as a resounding call to remember our divine nature amidst the transient nature of human existence. It reminds us that the physical body is merely a temporary vessel, and our true essence transcends the boundaries of birth and death.

In embracing this mantra, we embark on a journey to reconnect with the eternal within us, transcending the limitations of our mortal selves.

Lord Shiva: The Embodiment of Immortality

Central to the Maha Mrityunjaya Mantra is Lord Shiva, the embodiment of the immortal spirit. Lord Shiva is revered as the supreme deity in Hinduism, representing the cosmic consciousness and the transformative power of destruction and creation.

Lord Shiva is often depicted as the "Adiyogi," the first yogi, who dwells in deep meditation in the snowy peaks of the Himalayas. Through his unswerving devotion and mastery of the self, he exemplifies the eternal flame within every being, guiding us on our quest for self-realization.

Unlocking the Doors of Consciousness

The Maha Mrityunjaya Mantra serves as a key to unlocking the doors of consciousness, facilitating the expansion of awareness and the dissolution of limiting beliefs. As we immerse ourselves in the vibrations of this sacred mantra, it penetrates the layers of our subconscious mind, unearthing dormant potentials and illuminating the path towards self-discovery.

This mantra resonates with the divine energy that sustains and permeates all aspects of creation. By chanting it with sincerity and reverence, we establish a direct channel of communication with the divine realms, dissolving the illusion of separation and allowing the immortal essence to shine forth.

The Transformative Journey Ahead

As we embark on this transformative journey through the Maha Mrityunjaya Mantra, we shall explore the depths of its ancient wisdom and timeless significance. We shall delve into the meaning and essence of each word, uncovering the layers of mystical insight concealed within.

Furthermore, we shall embark on a practical exploration of this mantra, understanding the proper techniques, and guidelines for chanting it with precision and devotion. We shall also discover the multitude of benefits that arise from regular practice, including physical healing, mental clarity, emotional balance, and spiritual elevation.

Throughout this book, we shall intertwine the spiritual with the scientific, drawing upon modern research and understanding to validate the profound impact of mantras and sacred vibrations on our well-being. We shall delve into the symbiotic relationship between sound, consciousness, and the cosmos, bridging the ancient wisdom with contemporary knowledge.

Together, let us venture into the depths of our own being, guided by the resounding vibrations of the Maha Mrityunjaya Mantra. Let us awaken the immortal within and embrace the timeless truth that awaits us. The journey begins now, and the possibilities are infinite.

Chapter 2
The Immortal Within: Unleashing Your Potential

Deep within the fabric of our existence, beyond the ephemeral nature of our physical forms, lies an eternal essence - an immortal spark that yearns to be awakened. In this chapter, we embark on a profound exploration of the immortal within, unravelling the layers of our being to unleash the boundless potential that resides within each of us.

Beyond Mortal Constraints

As human beings, we often find ourselves entangled in the limitations of our mortal existence. We identify with our bodies, our thoughts, and our emotions, perceiving ourselves as finite beings bound by time and space. However, beneath these temporal veils lies a deeper truth—a truth that whispers of our inherent divinity and the eternal nature of our being.

The Illusion of Separation

One of the greatest illusions we face is the belief that we are separate from the universal consciousness that permeates all of existence. This illusion feeds into our fears, insecurities, and limitations, hindering us from accessing our full potential. Yet, when we recognize the interconnectedness of all beings and embrace the eternal essence within us, the illusion of separation begins to dissipate, giving way to a profound sense of unity and empowerment.

Remembering Our Divine Heritage

The call to awaken the immortal within is a call to remember our divine heritage - to reconnect with the source from which we have emanated. In this remembrance, we recognize that we are not mere mortals, but divine beings on a journey of self-discovery and self-realization.

Ancient wisdom traditions have long emphasized that our essence is not confined to the boundaries of our physical bodies. We are spiritual beings having a human experience, temporarily inhabiting these earthly forms. By acknowledging and honouring our divine nature, we open the floodgates of infinite possibilities and unleash the latent powers that lie dormant within us.

Embracing Our Infinite Potential

Unleashing our potential requires us to step beyond the limitations of our comfort zones and societal conditioning. It necessitates a shift in perspective—a shift from perceiving ourselves as finite beings to recognizing the infinite wellspring of creativity, wisdom, and love that flows within us.

Through practices such as meditation, introspection, and self-inquiry, we gain access to the depths of our consciousness, unearthing hidden talents, dormant abilities, and untapped reserves of strength. We realize that the power to shape our reality resides within us, waiting to be harnessed and expressed.

Transcending the Fear of Impermanence

One of the primary obstacles we encounter on our path to unleashing our potential is the fear of impermanence and the transient nature of life. Our mortal minds cling to the familiar, resisting change and the unknown. However, when we embrace the understanding that our essence is eternal and interconnected with the vast tapestry of creation, we can transcend this fear.

By recognizing that change is an inherent aspect of existence, we learn to flow with the currents of life, adapting and evolving with grace and resilience. We understand that true immortality lies not in the preservation of our physical forms, but in the legacy we leave behind and the transformative impact we have on the lives of others.

Embodying our Divine Gifts

As we embark on the journey of unleashing our potential, it is crucial to embrace and embody our unique gifts and talents. Each of us possesses a distinct combination of strengths, passions, and abilities that contribute to the tapestry of humanity. By acknowledging and nurturing these gifts, we align ourselves with our true purpose and find fulfilment in expressing our authentic selves.

Moreover, as we tap into our individual potential, we also recognize the interconnectedness of all beings. We understand that our growth and expansion are not isolated endeavours but contribute to the collective awakening of humanity. By shining our light brightly, we inspire others to awaken their own immortal essence and unleash their boundless potential.

The Path of Self-Realization

The journey of unleashing our potential is intricately intertwined with the path of self-realization—the process of knowing ourselves at the deepest level. It is a journey of self-discovery, introspection, and inner transformation.

Through practices such as self-reflection, mindfulness, and spiritual disciplines, we peel away the layers of conditioning, limiting beliefs, and societal expectations that have obscured our true nature. We dive into the depths of our being, encountering the shadows and embracing the light, as we come face to face with the immortality that resides within us.

As we progress on this path, we cultivate qualities such as self-awareness, compassion, and wisdom. We learn to navigate the challenges and obstacles that arise, recognizing them as opportunities for growth and transformation. And as we align ourselves with the immortal within, we become beacons of inspiration, guiding others on their own journey of self-realization.

Embracing the Journey

The journey of unleashing our potential is not a destination but a lifelong exploration - an ever-unfolding process of self-discovery and expansion. It requires patience, dedication, and a willingness to embrace the unknown.

As we traverse this path, we may encounter setbacks, doubts, and moments of uncertainty. Yet, it is in these moments that we are called to reconnect with the immortal essence within us, reminding ourselves of our inherent divinity and unwavering potential.

Embracing the journey of unleashing our potential is an act of surrender—an act of surrendering to the wisdom, guidance, and transformative power of the immortal within. It is an invitation to step into the fullness of who we truly are and embrace the limitless possibilities that await us.

As we continue our exploration, let us delve deeper into the practices, techniques, and wisdom that will enable us to unleash our potential and awaken the immortal essence that resides within us. The adventure awaits, and the infinite awaits our embrace.

In the realm of spiritual practices, mantras hold a significant place as sacred gateways to the divine. In this chapter, we delve into the profound world of mantras, exploring their origins, their significance, and their transformative power in connecting us to the divine realms.

Understanding Mantras

A mantra is a sacred sound, syllable, word, or phrase that carries a deep vibrational resonance. It is often chanted, recited, or repeated as a means of focusing the mind, invoking divine energies, and attuning oneself to higher states of consciousness.

The word "mantra" is derived from Sanskrit, with "man" meaning "mind" and "tra" meaning "instrument" or "tool." Thus, a mantra can be understood as a tool for harnessing the power of the mind and channelling it towards spiritual awakening and communion with the divine.

The Power of Sound

Sound has always played a significant role in spiritual practices across cultures and traditions. It is believed that sound carries energy and has the power to create, transform, and heal. In the context of mantras, sound becomes a vehicle for accessing and embodying divine energies.

Just as different musical notes and melodies evoke different emotions, mantras resonate with specific frequencies that correspond to different aspects of the divine. By chanting or reciting mantras, we attune ourselves to these sacred vibrations, aligning our beings with the cosmic harmonies that underpin the universe.

Origins of Mantras

The practice of using mantras dates back thousands of years and can be traced to ancient civilizations such as the Vedic culture of India. Mantras were revered as powerful tools for spiritual evolution, passed down through generations of sages and yogis.

In addition to their historical origins, mantras are often said to originate from the realm of the divine itself. They are considered to be divine revelations, imparted to enlightened beings through deep states of meditation and communion with higher consciousness.

Sanskrit: The Language of Mantras

Many mantras are expressed in Sanskrit, an ancient language that carries a profound vibrational potency. Sanskrit is revered as a sacred language, believed to have been created by the divine for the purpose of expressing the cosmic truths of existence.

The Sanskrit language is rich in its phonetic precision, with each syllable and sound meticulously crafted to evoke specific energies and meanings. Chanting mantras in Sanskrit not only invokes the vibrational power of the mantra itself but also connects us to the wisdom and lineage of those who have chanted these mantras for centuries.

The Essence of Mantras

At the heart of every mantra lies a sacred intention—an intention to awaken, transform, and align with divine consciousness. Each mantra carries a unique energy signature, resonating with specific qualities of the divine, such as love, healing, abundance, or spiritual illumination.

Through regular practice, chanting mantras creates a vibrational resonance within us that gradually dissolves the veils of ignorance and illusion. It purifies our thoughts, elevates our emotions, and opens us to the limitless possibilities of spiritual growth and self-realization.

The Maha Mrityunjaya Mantra: Key to Immortality

Among the vast array of mantras, the Maha Mrityunjaya Mantra holds a revered place as a gateway to immortality. It encapsulates the essence of the eternal within its sacred vibrations, invoking the conqueror of death and guiding us towards the realization of our immortal nature.

Chanting the Maha Mrityunjaya Mantra with devotion and understanding creates a profound energetic shift within us. It awakens our consciousness to the inherent divinity that resides within, dispelling the fear of death and embracing the eternal truth of our existence.

The Science of Mantras

While mantras are steeped in ancient spiritual wisdom, their transformative power has also been studied and validated by modern scientific research. Sound therapy, for instance, has shown that specific frequencies and vibrations can positively impact our physical, mental, and emotional well-being.

Mantras, with their inherent vibrational qualities, have been found to induce a state of relaxation, reduce stress, and enhance overall health. The rhythmic repetition of mantras engages the parasympathetic nervous system, promoting a sense of calm and inner harmony.

Furthermore, studies in the field of quantum physics suggest that sound waves and vibrations can influence the subtle energetic field that permeates our existence. Chanting mantras, therefore, can be seen as a means of harmonizing our energetic being with the cosmic symphony of creation.

The Practice of Chanting Mantras

To fully harness the transformative power of mantras, it is important to approach their practice with reverence, sincerity, and mindfulness. Here are some key considerations when chanting mantras:

Intentions and Affirmations: Set clear intentions and affirmations before chanting a mantra. This helps to align your focus and channel your energy towards specific goals or qualities you wish to cultivate.

Pronunciation and Diction: Pay attention to the correct pronunciation and diction of the mantra. Each syllable carries its own significance and vibrational resonance, so it is important to chant with precision and clarity.

Repetition and Devotion: Engage in regular and dedicated practice, repeating the mantra with devotion and sincerity. The power of mantras accumulates over time, deepening your connection with the divine and amplifying their transformative effects.

Inner Focus and Visualization: Cultivate inner focus and visualization while chanting the mantra. Allow the vibrations to permeate your entire being, imagining the divine qualities and energies invoked by the mantra flowing through you.

Silence and Stillness: After chanting the mantra, spend some time in silence and stillness, allowing the vibrations to settle within you. Observe any shifts in your thoughts, emotions, or energetic state, and embrace the subtle transformations taking place.

As we dive deeper into the realm of mantras, let us embrace the transformative power they hold and explore the vast array of mantras that exist to connect us with the divine. Through the practice of chanting mantras, we open the door to limitless possibilities, spiritual growth, and communion with the sacred.

Chapter 4
The Maha Mrityunjaya Mantra: Meaning and Significance

In this chapter, we embark on a profound exploration of the Maha Mrityunjaya Mantra, unravelling its meaning, significance, and the transformative power it holds. This ancient mantra, also known as the Great Death-Conquering Mantra, carries within it the essence of immortality and the path to awakening the divine within.

The Sacred Invocation

The Maha Mrityunjaya Mantra is a potent invocation to Lord Shiva, the embodiment of transformation, regeneration, and transcendence. It is a prayer that seeks protection, healing, and liberation from the cycle of birth and death.

The mantra is often recited during times of adversity, illness, or when facing the inevitability of death. It serves as a reminder of the impermanence of life and the eternal truth that lies beyond the transient realm.

The Sacred Syllables

The Maha Mrityunjaya Mantra is composed of a series of sacred syllables that carry deep vibrational significance. The mantra is traditionally chanted as:

ॐ त्र्यम्बकं यजामहे सुगन्धिं पुष्टिवर्धनम्
उर्वारुकमिव बन्धनान्मृत्योर्मुक्षीय माऽमृतात्॥

"Om Tryambakam Yajamahe Sugandhim Pushti-Vardhanam
Urvarukamiva Bandhanan Mrityor Mukshiya Maamritat."

The Meaning of the Mantra

The Maha Mrityunjaya Mantra holds profound symbolism and meaning within its syllables. Let us explore the deeper significance of each line:

Om: The sacred syllable "Om" represents the primordial sound, the universal vibration that pervades all of creation. It is the cosmic vibration from which all life emerges and to which all life returns. Chanting "Om" aligns us with the divine consciousness and opens the gateway to higher states of awareness.

Tryambakam: This word refers to Lord Shiva, the three-eyed deity who represents the divine aspects of creation, preservation, and dissolution. Lord Shiva's third eye symbolizes the awakening of spiritual insight and the transcendence of duality. By invoking Lord Shiva through "Tryambakam," we seek his divine grace and guidance on our path of liberation.

Yajamahe: This word denotes the act of worship, surrender, and offering. By chanting "Yajamahe," we express our devotion, surrendering our egoistic attachments and seeking union with the divine. It is an invitation to be embraced by the transformative energies of Lord Shiva.

Sugandhim: This term translates to "the fragrance" or "the auspicious one." It symbolizes the divine qualities and virtues that emanate from Lord Shiva—qualities such as love, compassion, wisdom, and grace. Chanting "Sugandhim" invokes these qualities, allowing them to permeate our being and transform our consciousness.

Pushti-Vardhanam: This phrase signifies the nourishment and sustenance that Lord Shiva bestows upon us. It represents the abundance of life, the growth of spiritual virtues, and the expansion of consciousness. By chanting "Pushti-Vardhanam," we seek the divine blessings that nurture our spiritual evolution.

Urvarukamiva: This phrase draws upon the imagery of a ripe cucumber hanging from its vine. Just as the cucumber detaches from the vine at the right time, the seeker aspires to detach from the cycle of birth and death. It symbolizes liberation from the cycles of samsara, the eternal cycle of birth and death, and the realization of one's immortal essence.

Bandhanan: This term refers to bondage, representing the ties and limitations that bind us to the illusion of the material world. By chanting "Bandhanan," we seek release from these bonds, freeing ourselves from the illusions of ego, attachment, and the fear of death.

Mrityor Mukshiya: These words embody the desire for liberation from the grip of death. "Mrityor" signifies death, and "Mukshiya" represents liberation or freedom. Chanting "Mrityor Mukshiya" is an invocation to transcend the limitations of mortality and awaken the immortal essence within.

Maamritat: This word signifies the nectar of immortality. By chanting "Maamritat," we seek to partake in the divine nectar that grants eternal life, transcending the limitations of the physical body and merging with the immortal consciousness.

The Healing and Transformative Power

The Maha Mrityunjaya Mantra carries within it a profound healing and transformative power. Through the repetition and contemplation of its sacred syllables, we align ourselves with the divine energies and qualities it represents.

The mantra serves as a potent antidote to the fear of death and the limitations of the physical body. It reminds us that our true essence is eternal and infinite, transcending the boundaries of time and space.

By chanting the mantra with devotion and understanding, we tap into the reservoir of divine energy, purify our consciousness, and awaken our innate capacity for self-healing and self-transformation.

The vibrational resonance of the Maha Mrityunjaya Mantra creates a harmonious balance within our energetic being, promoting physical, mental, and spiritual well-being. It purifies our thoughts, elevates our emotions, and restores our connection with the divine source.

Furthermore, the mantra serves as a powerful tool for spiritual growth and self-realization. It invites us to go beyond the limitations of the egoistic mind and embrace the eternal truth of our existence.

By surrendering to the vibrations of the mantra, we open ourselves to divine guidance, wisdom, and the unfoldment of our higher consciousness.

The Practice of Chanting the Maha Mrityunjaya Mantra

To fully experience the transformative power of the Maha Mrityunjaya Mantra, it is essential to engage in regular and dedicated practice. Here are some guidelines for incorporating the mantra into your spiritual journey:

Create a Sacred Space: Find a quiet and serene space where you can chant the mantra without distractions. Set up an altar or sacred space with symbols that resonate with Lord Shiva or the divine presence you connect with.

Set an Intention: Before chanting the mantra, set a clear intention for your practice. It could be healing, protection, spiritual growth, or any other specific intention aligned with your spiritual journey.

Choose a Chanting Technique: There are different ways to chant the Maha Mrityunjaya Mantra. You can recite it silently in your mind, chant it softly, or sing it aloud. Experiment with different techniques and find the one that resonates with you.

Practice with Mala Beads: Consider using a mala (prayer beads) to count the repetitions of the mantra. This helps to maintain focus and create a meditative rhythm in your chanting.

Engage in Japa Meditation: Japa meditation is the practice of repeating the mantra with focused awareness. As you chant the mantra, immerse yourself in its vibrations, and let go of distractions. Be fully present with each repetition, allowing the mantra to permeate your entire being.

Practice Regularly: Dedicate a specific time each day for your chanting practice. Consistency is key in harnessing the full transformative potential of the mantra. Even a few minutes of dedicated practice each day can yield profound results over time.

Reflect and Contemplate: After chanting the mantra, spend a few moments in silence, reflecting on the vibrations and insights that arise. Contemplate the meaning of the mantra and its relevance to your life journey. Allow the mantra to guide you towards deeper self-understanding and spiritual awakening.

Remember, the Maha Mrityunjaya Mantra is not just a collection of syllables, but a sacred invocation that carries the power to awaken the immortal essence within. Approach its practice with reverence, devotion, and an open heart, and let its transformative vibrations guide you on the path of self-discovery and spiritual evolution.

In the next chapter, we will explore the profound effects of the Maha Mrityunjaya Mantra on the mind, body, and spirit, and how it can bring healing and wholeness to our lives.

Chapter 5
<u>Chanting the Maha Mrityunjaya Mantra: Technique and Benefits</u>

In this chapter, we delve into the practice of chanting the Maha Mrityunjaya Mantra, exploring various techniques and the abundant benefits it offers. As we engage in the rhythmic repetition of this sacred mantra, we tap into its transformative power and unlock the doors to healing, spiritual growth, and inner awakening.

Preparation for Chanting

Before beginning your chanting practice, it is important to create a conducive environment that promotes focus, relaxation, and reverence. Here are some suggestions for preparing yourself:

Choose a Quiet Space: Find a calm and quiet space where you can chant without interruptions. It could be a dedicated meditation corner in your home, a serene outdoor location, or any place where you feel comfortable and at peace.

Create a Sacred Atmosphere: Arrange your sacred space with meaningful symbols or images that represent the divine, such as pictures of Lord Shiva, candles, flowers, or other objects that resonate with your spiritual connection. This helps to create an atmosphere of devotion and reverence.

Set an Intention: Before you begin chanting, take a moment to set a clear intention for your practice. It could be healing, spiritual growth, inner peace, or any other specific intention that aligns with your needs and aspirations.

Relax and Ground Yourself: Take a few deep breaths and consciously release any tension or distractions. Allow your body and mind to relax, grounding yourself in the present moment.

Chanting Techniques

There are different ways to chant the Maha Mrityunjaya Mantra, and you can choose the technique that resonates with you. Here are three common techniques:

Repetition with Mindful Focus: Sit comfortably in an upright position, close your eyes, and take a few deep breaths to center yourself. Begin chanting the mantra, either silently or aloud, focusing your attention on the sound and vibration of each syllable. Let go of any distractions that arise and bring your mind back to the mantra whenever it wanders.

Japa Meditation with Mala Beads: Hold a mala (prayer beads) in your right hand and start moving the beads, one by one, as you repeat the mantra. Begin with the bead next to the guru bead (the larger central bead), using your thumb and middle finger to move the beads.

Chant the mantra softly or silently as you move through each bead. Continue until you have completed one full round or a specific number of repetitions.

Chanting with Music: You can enhance your chanting experience by incorporating soothing music or chanting along with recorded versions of the Maha Mrityunjaya Mantra. Choose music that resonates with your heart and enhances the devotional aspect of your practice.

Allow the melodies and rhythms to guide your chanting, immersing yourself fully in the experience.

Benefits of Chanting the Maha Mrityunjaya Mantra

The Maha Mrityunjaya Mantra is a powerful tool for self-transformation and spiritual awakening. Its vibrations resonate deep within our being, bringing about numerous benefits on multiple levels. Let us explore some of the profound benefits of regular chanting:

Healing and Well-being: The mantra's vibrational energy has a harmonizing effect on our physical, mental, and emotional states. It helps to release stress, balance the nervous system, and promote overall well-being. Chanting the Maha Mrityunjaya Mantra can assist in healing physical ailments, reducing anxiety, and cultivating inner peace.

Protection and Liberation: The mantra serves as a protective shield, invoking the divine energies that safeguard us from negative influences and obstacles on our spiritual path. It helps to dissolve karmic patterns, release attachments, and liberate us from the cycles of suffering and ignorance.

Awakening of Consciousness: As we chant the Maha Mrityunjaya Mantra, we awaken dormant aspects of our consciousness. The mantra's vibrations penetrate the layers of conditioning and limited beliefs, expanding our awareness and opening us up to higher realms of existence.

It can lead to profound insights, spiritual growth, and a deepened connection with our true essence.

Transformation and Inner Alchemy: The repetitive chanting of the mantra facilitates a process of inner alchemy, transmuting lower energies into higher vibrations. It purifies our thoughts, emotions, and intentions, fostering qualities such as compassion, love, and wisdom.

This transformational journey brings us closer to our divine nature and ignites the flame of self-realization.

Cultivation of Devotion and Surrender: Chanting the Maha Mrityunjaya Mantra cultivates a sense of devotion and surrender to the divine. It deepens our connection with the spiritual realm and nurtures a loving relationship with the source of all creation.

Through devotion and surrender, we find solace, guidance, and profound inner peace.

Integrating Chanting into Daily Life

To fully embrace the benefits of chanting the Maha Mrityunjaya Mantra, it is beneficial to integrate it into your daily life. Here are some suggestions on how to do so:

Morning Practice: Begin your day with a chanting session, setting a positive tone for the hours ahead. Dedicate a few minutes to chanting the mantra, allowing its vibrations to uplift your spirit and align your intentions with the divine.

Meditative Breaks: Take short breaks throughout the day to reconnect with the mantra. Find moments of stillness, whether during a lunch break, while commuting, or in nature, to chant the Maha Mrityunjaya Mantra silently or softly. These mini-meditative breaks can help restore balance and bring a sense of peace amidst daily activities.

Bedtime Ritual: Before going to sleep, engage in a quiet chanting practice. Reflect on the day's experiences, offer gratitude, and chant the mantra to release any residual tensions and surrender to the healing energies of the divine.

Group Chanting: Join or initiate group chanting sessions with like-minded individuals. The collective energy amplifies the potency of the mantra and fosters a sense of unity, support, and spiritual community.

Deepening Your Connection with the Mantra

As you progress on your journey of chanting the Maha Mrityunjaya Mantra, you may feel a deepening connection with its essence. Here are some additional practices to deepen your relationship with the mantra:

Study and Contemplation: Explore the sacred texts, commentaries, and teachings related to the Maha Mrityunjaya Mantra. Delve into its symbolism, philosophy, and spiritual significance. Reflect on its meaning and contemplate how its wisdom can be integrated into your daily life.

Journaling: Maintain a spiritual journal to record your experiences, insights, and reflections during and after chanting sessions. This practice helps to deepen your understanding, track your progress, and gain clarity on the transformative effects of the mantra.

Seek Guidance: If needed, seek guidance from a knowledgeable teacher or spiritual mentor who can provide insights and support on your journey with the Maha Mrityunjaya Mantra. Their guidance can help you navigate any challenges and offer valuable perspectives on the practice.

Trust Your Intuition: As you deepen your relationship with the Maha Mrityunjaya Mantra, trust your intuition and inner guidance. Allow yourself to be guided by the wisdom that unfolds within you, as the mantra reveals its transformative power in your life.

Chapter 6
Immortality in Ancient Texts and Mythology

In this chapter, we embark on a journey through the rich tapestry of ancient texts and mythology, exploring the concept of immortality. From the mythological realms of gods and goddesses to the profound wisdom of ancient scriptures, we delve into the multifaceted expressions of immortality and its significance in human consciousness.

Immortal Beings in Mythology

Across various mythologies and folklore, we encounter stories of immortal beings who transcend the boundaries of time and mortality. These mythical figures embody the yearning for eternal life and serve as powerful symbols of divine essence within the human experience.

Greek Mythology: In Greek mythology, we encounter the gods and goddesses of Mount Olympus, who possess immortality and dwell in a realm beyond mortal limitations. Figures such as Zeus, Hera, Poseidon, and Athena are revered as immortal beings, embodying divine attributes and serving as archetypes of power, wisdom, and beauty.

Hindu Mythology: Hindu mythology is replete with tales of gods and goddesses who are considered immortal. Deities like Lord Vishnu, Lord Shiva, and Devi Parvati are regarded as eternal beings who exist beyond the cycles of birth and death. Their divine qualities and actions inspire devotion and represent the possibility of transcending mortal limitations.

Norse Mythology: In Norse mythology, the gods and goddesses, including Odin, Thor, and Freya, are revered as immortals who reside in realms like Asgard. They possess superhuman abilities and play significant roles in the cosmic order, embodying both the light and dark aspects of existence.

These mythological narratives not only captivate our imagination but also reflect our innate desire for immortality and the yearning to connect with the divine aspects of our own being.

Immortality in Ancient Texts

The pursuit of immortality is also reflected in ancient spiritual texts and scriptures from various cultures. These texts offer profound insights into the nature of existence, the quest for eternal life, and the awakening of the immortal essence within.

Vedas and Upanishads: The Vedas and Upanishads, ancient Indian scriptures, contain philosophical and spiritual teachings that explore the nature of immortality. They discuss the concept of the Atman, the eternal soul, and its connection to the ultimate reality, Brahman. These texts emphasize the realization of one's true nature as the key to transcending the cycles of birth and death.

Egyptian Book of the Dead: The Egyptian Book of the Dead, a collection of ancient funerary texts, provides insights into the Egyptian belief in the afterlife and the quest for immortality. It contains rituals, spells, and instructions for navigating the journey of the soul beyond death and attaining eternal life in the realm of Osiris.

Taoist Texts: Taoist philosophy, as expounded in texts like the Tao Te Ching and the Zhuangzi, explores the path to immortality through the cultivation of inner harmony and alignment with the Tao, the eternal principle underlying all existence. These texts emphasize the transcendent power of living in harmony with nature and attaining spiritual enlightenment.

Epic of Gilgamesh: The Epic of Gilgamesh, an ancient Mesopotamian epic, tells the story of Gilgamesh's quest for immortality after the death of his dear friend, Enkidu. The epic explores themes of mortality, the fear of death, and the search for eternal life, ultimately conveying the wisdom that true immortality lies in leaving a lasting legacy and finding meaning in the present moment.

These ancient texts provide glimpses into the wisdom of our ancestors and offer profound insights into the human longing for immortality. They remind us that the quest for immortality is not merely a physical pursuit but a spiritual journey towards realizing our divine nature.

Symbolic Interpretations of Immortality

Beyond the literal interpretations, the concept of immortality carries symbolic significance that resonates with our spiritual and personal growth. It invites us to explore the depths of our being and unlock the immortal essence within.

Inner Transformation: Immortality can be seen as a metaphor for inner transformation and spiritual evolution. It represents the journey of shedding our limited identities and aligning with our true nature, which is timeless and eternal. Through practices such as meditation, self-reflection, and selfless service, we can transcend the constraints of ego and connect with the infinite wellspring of our being.

Legacy and Influence: Immortality can also be understood in terms of the lasting impact we make in the world. It is not necessarily about physical longevity but about the enduring imprint we leave on others' lives and the collective consciousness. By cultivating virtues, sharing wisdom, and engaging in acts of kindness and compassion, we can contribute to a legacy that continues to inspire and uplift future generations.

Connection with the Divine: Immortality signifies our innate connection with the divine source of all life. It reminds us that we are not separate from the eternal energy that permeates the universe but are interconnected with it. By nurturing our spiritual connection through prayer, devotion, and self-realization, we can experience glimpses of our own divine immortality.

As we explore the concept of immortality in ancient texts and mythology, we begin to recognize that it is not confined to the realm of fantasy or folklore but holds deeper truths about the nature of our existence.

It invites us to embrace our inherent divinity, engage in the transformative journey of self-discovery, and awaken the immortal essence within.

Chapter 7
Nada Yoga: The Yoga of Sound

In this chapter, we dive into the profound practice of Nada Yoga, also known as the Yoga of Sound. Nada, meaning "sound" in Sanskrit, refers to the subtle vibrations that permeate the universe. Nada Yoga explores the transformative power of sound and its ability to awaken higher states of consciousness, leading us on a journey of self-discovery and spiritual evolution.

Understanding Nada Yoga

Nada Yoga is rooted in the understanding that sound is not merely an auditory experience but a powerful tool for self-realization and inner transformation. It recognizes that all creation is a manifestation of sound and that by attuning ourselves to the subtle vibrations of the universe, we can harmonize our body, mind, and spirit.

In Nada Yoga, the human body is viewed as a microcosm reflecting the macrocosm of the universe. Just as the universe is composed of vibrations, so too are our bodies. By becoming aware of and aligning ourselves with the cosmic vibrations, we can tap into the inherent wisdom and power that resides within us.

The Power of Sacred Sound

Sacred sound has been revered across cultures and spiritual traditions as a means to connect with the divine and attain higher states of consciousness. From the ancient chants of Vedic hymns to the recitation of mantras and the melodic tunes of devotional songs, sacred sound carries a vibrational energy that transcends language and touches the depths of our being.

Sound has the power to create, sustain, and dissolve. It can uplift and inspire, heal and harmonize, and even invoke mystical experiences. Through the practice of Nada Yoga, we harness the transformative potential of sacred sound to awaken our dormant faculties, expand our awareness, and experience the unity of existence.

Nada Yoga Practices

Nada Yoga encompasses a variety of practices that enable us to cultivate a deeper connection with the divine through sound.

Here are a few key practices:

Mantra Chanting: Chanting sacred mantras is one of the most common and powerful practices in Nada Yoga. Mantras are potent sound vibrations that carry specific energies and meanings. By repetitively chanting mantras, we attune our mind and body to their transformative vibrations, purifying our consciousness and opening ourselves to higher states of awareness.

Pranayama and Sound: Pranayama, the practice of breath control, can be combined with sound to deepen our experience in Nada Yoga. By integrating specific sounds, such as the chanting of Om or other sacred syllables, with controlled breathing, we harmonize the flow of prana (life force energy) within us, activating subtle energy centers and expanding our consciousness.

Listening Meditation: In this practice, we cultivate deep listening, directing our attention to the sounds that arise within and around us. By observing the sounds without judgment or attachment, we enter a state of deep presence and awareness. This practice helps to quiet the mind, dissolve distractions, and attune ourselves to the subtle vibrations of existence.

Nada Sankirtan: Nada Sankirtan refers to the collective singing or chanting of devotional songs or bhajans. This practice fosters a sense of unity and community, amplifying the vibrations of sacred sound. Through the shared experience of sound, we uplift our hearts, dissolve the boundaries of ego, and immerse ourselves in the ocean of divine love.

Benefits of Nada Yoga

The practice of Nada Yoga offers numerous benefits for our physical, mental, and spiritual well-being. Some of these benefits include:

Enhanced Concentration and Focus: Regular practice of Nada Yoga improves our ability to concentrate and focus. As we attune our mind to the subtle vibrations of sound, distractions diminish, and our awareness becomes centered and single-pointed.

Stress Reduction and Relaxation: The soothing and harmonizing effects of sacred sound have a profound impact on our nervous system. Nada Yoga practices help to release tension, reduce stress, and induce a state of deep relaxation, promoting overall well-being and balance.

Heightened Intuition and Inner Wisdom: Through the practice of Nada Yoga, we refine our sensitivity to subtle energies and vibrations. This heightened sensitivity enhances our intuition, allowing us to access deeper levels of insight and inner wisdom.

Awakening of Spiritual Potential: Nada Yoga serves as a catalyst for spiritual growth and self-realization. By aligning ourselves with the cosmic vibrations, we awaken dormant aspects of our being, expand our consciousness, and connect with our true nature.

Integrating Nada Yoga into Daily Life

To fully embrace the transformative power of Nada Yoga, it is essential to integrate its principles and practices into our daily lives. Here are some suggestions on how to do so:

Sacred Sound in Daily Activities: Infuse your daily activities with sacred sound. Whether it's humming a mantra while cooking, reciting a prayer while walking, or listening to uplifting music during your commute, find ways to incorporate sound that nourishes your soul and uplifts your spirit.

Regular Chanting Practice: Dedicate a specific time each day to engage in mantra chanting or devotional singing. Create a sacred space where you can immerse yourself in the vibrations of sound and connect with the divine presence within you.

Mindful Listening: Cultivate a practice of mindful listening throughout the day. Pay attention to the sounds around you, both in nature and in your immediate environment. Observe the effects that different sounds have on your state of being and use them as a reminder of the underlying vibrations of existence.

Sound Healing Practices: Explore sound healing modalities such as Tibetan singing bowls, crystal bowls, or tuning forks. These instruments produce specific frequencies and vibrations that can harmonize and balance your energy system, supporting your overall well-being.

By integrating Nada Yoga into our daily lives, we awaken our capacity to perceive the divine essence that permeates all of creation. We align ourselves with the rhythms of the universe, attune our consciousness to the sacred vibrations of sound, and embark on a transformative journey of self-discovery and spiritual evolution.

Chapter 8
<u>Sacred Vibration Frequencies and Healing</u>

In this chapter, we delve into the profound connection between sacred vibration frequencies and healing. Throughout history, various cultures and spiritual traditions have recognized the therapeutic power of sound and vibrations in promoting physical, emotional, and spiritual well-being.

We explore how sacred vibration frequencies can be harnessed for healing and transformation.

The Science of Vibration and Resonance

To understand the healing potential of sacred vibration frequencies, it is important to grasp the fundamental principles of vibration and resonance. Everything in the universe, from the smallest particles to the grandest celestial bodies, is in a state of vibration. These vibrations create distinct frequencies that shape the nature and characteristics of each entity.

Resonance occurs when one vibrating object or frequency synchronizes with another, creating a harmonic relationship. When two objects resonate, they amplify each other's vibrations, leading to a greater intensity and coherence of energy. This phenomenon of resonance is at the core of the healing potential of sacred vibration frequencies.

The Role of Sacred Vibration Frequencies in Healing

Sacred vibration frequencies have been used for centuries as a means of promoting healing on multiple levels.

Here are some key aspects of their healing potential:

Restoring Balance and Harmony: When we experience physical or emotional distress, it is often a result of an imbalance or disharmony within our energetic system. Sacred vibration frequencies have the ability to restore balance and harmony by entraining our energy field to their coherent vibrations. Through resonance, these frequencies can help realign our physical, emotional, and spiritual aspects, promoting overall well-being.

Dissolving Energetic Blockages: Energetic blockages, such as stagnant or imbalanced energy, can manifest as physical or emotional ailments. Sacred vibration frequencies have the power to dissolve these blockages by creating resonance and facilitating the free flow of energy throughout our system. This can lead to the release of stored tension and the restoration of vitality.

Cellular Healing and DNA Activation: The human body is composed of trillions of cells, each vibrating at its unique frequency. Sacred vibration frequencies can penetrate at the cellular level, promoting healing and activating the body's innate regenerative abilities. This process can positively influence gene expression and promote overall cellular health and vitality.

Emotional Release and Transformation: Emotions are energy in motion, and when emotions become stagnant or suppressed, they can lead to imbalances and dis-ease. Sacred vibration frequencies can facilitate the release and transformation of emotional energy, creating a space for emotional healing, catharsis, and inner transformation.

Sound Healing Modalities

Various sound healing modalities harness sacred vibration frequencies to facilitate healing and well-being.

Here are some commonly used modalities:

Tibetan Singing Bowls: Tibetan singing bowls produce a rich blend of harmonic frequencies that can induce a deep state of relaxation and balance. The vibrations emitted by these bowls resonate with our energy centers (chakras), promoting their alignment and restoring harmony within the body-mind system.

Crystal Singing Bowls: Crystal singing bowls, made from quartz crystals, produce pure and powerful tones that resonate with different frequencies. Each bowl corresponds to a specific chakra or energy center, allowing for targeted healing and balancing of the corresponding aspects of our being.

Tuning Forks: Tuning forks are precision-crafted instruments that emit specific frequencies when struck or activated. By placing tuning forks on or near the body, we can direct the vibrations to specific areas, promoting healing and energetic alignment.

Vocal Toning and Chanting: Our own voice is a potent instrument for healing. Vocal toning involves producing sustained vocal sounds that resonate within the body, promoting relaxation, release, and energetic alignment. Chanting sacred mantras or devotional songs also harnesses the power of sound and vibration to evoke healing and transformation.

Integrating Sacred Vibration Frequencies into Healing Practices

The integration of sacred vibration frequencies into healing practices can greatly enhance their efficacy.

Here are some ways to incorporate these frequencies into your healing journey:

Intentional Listening: Dedicate time to listening to recorded or live performances of sacred chants, mantras, or sound healing sessions. Create a serene and sacred space where you can fully immerse yourself in the vibrations and allow them to permeate your entire being.

Personalized Sound Healing Sessions: Seek out professional sound healers or therapists who can provide personalized sound healing sessions using modalities such as singing bowls, tuning forks, or vocal toning. These sessions can target specific areas of concern and facilitate deep healing and transformation.

Self-Expression through Sound: Explore your own voice as a tool for healing. Engage in vocal toning, chanting, or singing as a means of releasing emotions, finding inner resonance, and promoting self-healing.

Sound Baths and Group Healing Sessions: Participate in sound baths or group healing sessions where multiple instruments and voices come together to create a symphony of sacred vibrations. The collective resonance amplifies the healing effects and creates a powerful container for transformation.

By incorporating sacred vibration frequencies into our healing practices, we tap into the inherent wisdom and power of sound to promote holistic well-being. These frequencies can assist us in restoring balance, releasing stagnant energies, and accessing deeper levels of healing and transformation.

Chapter 9
Science of Mantra: A Modern Perspective

In this chapter, we delve into the fascinating field of the science of mantra from a modern perspective. Mantras have been revered for centuries as potent tools for transformation and spiritual awakening. However, with advancements in science and technology, we now have the opportunity to explore the effects of mantras on the human mind and body through a scientific lens.

We uncover the scientific principles behind the power of mantras and their impact on our well-being.

The Power of Sound and Vibrations

Sound and vibrations have a profound influence on our physical and mental states. Scientific research has shown that specific sound frequencies can impact brainwave patterns, heart rate, and even the expression of genes. The human body is a complex system of vibrations, and when we engage with specific sound frequencies, we can stimulate and harmonize these vibrations, leading to various physiological and psychological effects.

The Effects of Mantras on Brainwaves

Recent studies utilizing electroencephalography (EEG) have provided insights into the effects of mantras on brainwave activity. Mantras have been found to induce a state of focused attention and heightened awareness, leading to increased alpha and theta brainwave activity. These brainwave patterns are associated with deep relaxation, creativity, and enhanced states of consciousness.

The rhythmic repetition of mantras is thought to activate the frontal cortex of the brain, promoting clarity of thought, concentration, and a sense of calm. Mantras have also been found to reduce the activity of the default mode network (DMN), which is associated with mind-wandering and self-referential thoughts. By quieting the DMN, mantras help to bring about a state of present-moment awareness and inner stillness.

Mantras and the Vagus Nerve

The vagus nerve, the longest nerve in the human body, plays a crucial role in regulating various bodily functions and influencing our overall well-being. Recent studies have shown that the rhythmic chanting of mantras can stimulate the vagus nerve, leading to a cascade of physiological responses known as the relaxation response.

When the vagus nerve is activated, it triggers the release of neurotransmitters such as acetylcholine and gamma-aminobutyric acid (GABA), which promote relaxation, reduce stress, and enhance feelings of well-being. This activation of the vagus nerve through mantra chanting has been linked to improved cardiovascular health, reduced inflammation, and increased resilience to stress.

The Mind-Body Connection

The mind-body connection is a well-established concept in modern science, highlighting the intricate relationship between our thoughts, emotions, and physical well-being. Mantras serve as a bridge between the mind and body, as the vibrations created by chanting or reciting mantras have the power to influence our mental and emotional states, which, in turn, can impact our physical health.

Studies have shown that the repetition of mantras can lead to a decrease in stress hormones, such as cortisol, and an increase in the production of endorphins, which are natural pain-relieving and mood-enhancing substances.

The positive psychological effects of mantras, including reduced anxiety and improved mood, have been observed in various clinical settings.

The Placebo Effect and Belief

The placebo effect, whereby a person experiences a positive response to a treatment due to their belief in its effectiveness, is a well-documented phenomenon. Mantras, when approached with faith and belief, can harness the power of the placebo effect to promote healing and well-being.

The act of chanting or reciting mantras with intention and devotion can create a psychological and emotional state of receptivity, allowing for a deep sense of connection with the divine or higher consciousness. This connection can activate the body's innate healing mechanisms and amplify the healing effects of the mantra.

Practical Applications and Integration

The scientific understanding of mantras opens up a world of practical applications and integration into various aspects of our lives. Here are some ways to incorporate the science of mantras into your daily routine:

Meditation and Mindfulness: Use mantras as a focal point during meditation or mindfulness practices. The rhythmic repetition of a mantra can help anchor your attention and cultivate a state of present-moment awareness.

Stress Reduction and Relaxation: Employ mantras as a tool for stress reduction and relaxation. Chanting or listening to soothing mantras can activate the relaxation response, calm the nervous system, and promote a sense of tranquillity.

Affirmations and Positive Self-Talk: Harness the power of mantras as affirmations or positive self-talk. Choose empowering statements that resonate with you and repeat them regularly to reprogram your subconscious mind and cultivate a positive mindset.

Healing Practices: Integrate mantras into your healing practices, such as yoga, energy healing, or any modality that supports your well-being. The vibrational qualities of mantras can enhance the healing process and deepen the therapeutic effects.

As we continue to explore the science of mantras, we unlock a deeper understanding of their profound impact on our physical, mental, and spiritual well-being. The integration of this knowledge with traditional wisdom allows us to tap into the transformative power of mantras in a way that is accessible, relevant, and beneficial in our modern lives.

Chapter 10
Mantra Meditation: Deepening Your Practice

In this chapter, we delve into the art of mantra meditation and explore how we can deepen our practice to experience profound states of inner peace, clarity, and spiritual connection. Mantra meditation is a powerful technique that utilizes the repetition of sacred sounds or phrases to quiet the mind, awaken higher consciousness, and cultivate a deep sense of presence.

We will explore various aspects of mantra meditation and provide guidance on how to enhance your practice.

Setting the Stage for Mantra Meditation

Creating the right environment and mindset is essential for a fruitful mantra meditation practice.

Here are some key elements to consider:

Sacred Space: Designate a space in your home or any quiet area where you can practice mantra meditation regularly. Clear the space of any clutter and infuse it with elements that inspire a sense of tranquillity, such as candles, incense, or meaningful objects.

Comfortable Posture: Choose a posture that allows you to be relaxed yet alert. This can be sitting on a cushion with your legs crossed, sitting on a chair with your feet grounded, or any position that feels comfortable for an extended period. Ensure your spine is straight, allowing for a smooth flow of energy.

Time Commitment: Determine a consistent time commitment for your mantra meditation practice. Start with a manageable duration, such as 10-15 minutes, and gradually increase it as you become more comfortable. Consistency is key in establishing a deep and transformative practice.

Selecting a Mantra

Choosing the right mantra is crucial for your meditation practice. Here are some considerations:

Traditional Mantras: Traditional mantras, such as the Maha Mrityunjaya Mantra, have been passed down through generations and carry potent spiritual vibrations. These mantras have a rich history and are embedded with sacred energy.

Personal Affinity: Select a mantra that resonates with you on a personal level. It could be a mantra associated with a specific deity, a mantra that aligns with your intentions or spiritual path, or a mantra that evokes a particular quality or state of being you wish to cultivate.

Guidance from a Teacher: If you have a spiritual teacher or mentor, seek their guidance in selecting a mantra that is suitable for your unique journey. They can provide insights and recommend mantras based on their wisdom and experience.

Remember that the power of the mantra lies not only in the specific words but also in the intention and devotion with which it is practised. As you chant the mantra, allow its vibrations to permeate your being and invoke a deep sense of connection and reverence.

The Practice of Mantra Meditation

Here is a step-by-step guide to deepen your mantra meditation practice:

Preparation: Find a comfortable seated posture and take a few moments to center yourself. Close your eyes, take a few deep breaths, and bring your attention inward.

Grounding: Bring your awareness to your body and the sensation of contact with the ground or support beneath you. Feel rooted and grounded in the present moment.

Invocation: Begin by invoking the presence of the divine, the universal energy, or whatever higher power you resonate with. Offer your gratitude and set your intention for the meditation.

Chanting the Mantra: Start chanting the chosen mantra aloud or silently. Allow the rhythm and vibrations of the mantra to guide your focus and dissolve any distractions. Maintain a steady pace and let the mantra flow naturally.

Breath Awareness: Concurrently, bring your attention to the breath. Notice the inhales and exhales, the sensation of the breath flowing in and out of your body. Allow the breath to anchor you in the present moment.

Witnessing Thoughts: As you chant the mantra, thoughts and distractions may arise. Instead of resisting or engaging with them, adopt the role of a witness. Observe the thoughts without judgment and gently bring your focus back to the mantra and the breath.

Deepening the Experience: As your meditation deepens, you may experience moments of stillness, clarity, or heightened states of consciousness. Embrace these experiences without clinging to them, allowing them to come and go freely.

Completion and Integration: When you feel ready, gradually bring the mantra chanting to a close. Take a few moments to sit in silence, absorbing the effects of the practice. Offer gratitude for the opportunity to engage in mantra meditation and carry the sense of peace and presence into your day.

Deepening Your Practice

To deepen your mantra meditation practice, consider the following:

Regularity: Consistency is key in deepening any spiritual practice. Aim to meditate daily or at least on a regular schedule that works for you. As you build momentum, you will notice the transformative effects unfolding in your life.

Lengthening the Duration: Gradually increase the duration of your meditation sessions. Challenge yourself to sit for longer periods, allowing for deeper immersion in the mantra and the meditative state.

Silent Meditation: Experiment with silent mantra meditation, where you repeat the mantra mentally without vocalizing it. This practice can cultivate a deeper internalization and subtler experience of the mantra vibrations.

Group Meditation: Join group meditation sessions or retreats where you can chant mantras collectively. The collective energy enhances the potency of the practice and creates a supportive environment for spiritual growth.

Study and Reflection: Deepen your understanding of mantras by studying their meanings, symbolism, and cultural significance. Reflect on the teachings associated with the mantras you resonate with, exploring their philosophical and spiritual dimensions.

As you delve deeper into your mantra meditation practice, you will uncover new layers of awareness, connection, and inner transformation. Embrace the journey with an open heart and a receptive mind, allowing the power of the mantras to guide you on the path of self-discovery and spiritual awakening.

Chapter 11
<u>Manifesting Immortality: Applying the Mantra in Daily Life</u>

In this chapter, we explore how to apply the transformative power of the Maha Mrityunjaya Mantra in our daily lives to manifest immortality in a holistic sense. Immortality, in this context, refers to awakening our true essence, connecting with the divine, and living a life of purpose, vitality, and spiritual fulfilment.

We delve into practical ways to integrate the mantra into various aspects of our daily routines and empower ourselves to live in alignment with its sacred vibrations.

Cultivating Awareness and Presence

The first step in applying the Maha Mrityunjaya Mantra in daily life is to cultivate awareness and presence. By consciously bringing our attention to the present moment, we can fully engage with the opportunities and experiences that unfold before us. Here are some practices to support this:

Morning Reflection: Begin your day by reflecting on the mantra's meaning and significance. Set your intentions for the day, inviting the qualities of healing, protection, and transcendence into your thoughts and actions.

Mindful Activities: Infuse mindfulness into daily activities such as eating, walking, or performing household chores. Pay attention to the sensations, tastes, and smells, allowing yourself to fully immerse in the present moment.

Breathing with Mantra: Connect the rhythm of your breath with the mantra. As you inhale, silently repeat "Om Tryambakam" and as you exhale, silently repeat "Yajamahe, Sugandhim, Pushtivardhanam." This practice synchronizes your breath with the mantra's vibrations, grounding you in the present moment.

Applying the Mantra to Challenges

Life presents us with various challenges and obstacles. By applying the Maha Mrityunjaya Mantra during difficult times, we can access its transformative energy to navigate through adversity with resilience and grace. Here's how:

Chanting in Difficult Moments: When faced with challenges, take a moment to recite or chant the mantra. Allow its vibrations to soothe your mind, restore balance, and provide the strength to face obstacles with a sense of inner calm.

Mantra Affirmations: Create empowering affirmations using the essence of the mantra. For example, "I am protected, healed, and guided through life's challenges." Repeat these affirmations during challenging situations, anchoring yourself in the power of the mantra's vibrations.

Surrendering and Letting Go: Release attachment to the outcome and surrender to the divine flow. Trust that the mantra's vibrations are guiding you towards the highest good, even in the face of challenges. Allow the mantra to remind you of the impermanence of circumstances and the eternal nature of the soul.

Expressing Gratitude and Service

Gratitude and service are powerful ways to align with the divine essence within and manifest immortality in our daily lives. The Maha Mrityunjaya Mantra can inspire and amplify these qualities. Here's how to incorporate them:

Gratitude Practice: Cultivate a daily gratitude practice, expressing appreciation for the blessings in your life. As you recite the mantra, infuse it with gratitude, acknowledging the healing, protection, and abundance that surround you.

Selfless Service: Engage in acts of selfless service, offering your time, skills, or resources to support others. As you serve, hold the mantra's vibrations in your heart, dedicating your actions to the well-being and upliftment of all beings.

Loving-Kindness Meditation: Expand your practice to include loving-kindness meditation. As you recite phrases of loving-kindness, infuse them with the vibrations of the mantra, extending healing and blessings to yourself and all sentient beings.

Living with Purpose and Alignment

Living a life of purpose and alignment with our highest truth is a fundamental aspect of manifesting immortality. The Maha Mrityunjaya Mantra can guide us in discovering and embodying our unique purpose. Here's how to integrate it into this process:

Soulful Reflection: Engage in introspection and self-reflection to explore your passions, values, and deepest desires. Use the mantra as a guide, invoking its energy to connect with your soul's purpose and align your actions accordingly.

Meditation for Clarity: Practice mantra meditation specifically focusing on gaining clarity about your life's purpose. Ask for guidance and insight, allowing the mantra's vibrations to illuminate the path that aligns with your soul's journey.

Inspired Action: Take inspired action aligned with your purpose. Allow the mantra's vibrations to infuse your endeavours, reminding you of the eternal nature of your essence and the significance of your contribution to the world.

As you apply the Maha Mrityunjaya Mantra in your daily life, you will witness the unfolding of immortality within you. Embrace the journey with an open heart, trust in the transformative power of the mantra, and allow it to guide you towards a life of purpose, vitality, and spiritual fulfilment.

Chapter 12
Sacred Symbols and Yantras: Amplifying Divine Energies

In this chapter, we delve into the realm of sacred symbols and yantras, exploring their significance and the profound impact they have in amplifying the divine energies invoked through the Maha Mrityunjaya Mantra. Symbols have long been used as powerful tools to connect with higher consciousness, invoke spiritual energies, and awaken deep states of awareness.

We will explore the meaning and application of sacred symbols and yantras, and how they can enhance our practice and spiritual journey.

The Power of Symbols

Symbols hold a unique power to communicate profound truths and awaken deep states of consciousness. They transcend language barriers and speak directly to our intuitive and subconscious minds. When we engage with sacred symbols, we tap into their inherent energies and align ourselves with the divine vibrations they represent. Here are some key aspects of working with symbols:

Universal Language: Symbols carry universal meanings that transcend cultural and linguistic boundaries. They connect us to the collective consciousness and the wisdom of ancient civilizations. The Maha Mrityunjaya Mantra itself is a powerful symbol, representing the eternal cycle of life and death and our journey towards immortality.

Energetic Resonance: Symbols possess an energetic resonance that activates corresponding energies within us. When we interact with symbols, whether visually or through contemplation, we attune ourselves to their vibrations, awakening dormant aspects of our being and connecting with higher realms of consciousness.

Amplification of Intentions: Symbols act as amplifiers of intentions. When we combine the power of the Maha Mrityunjaya Mantra with sacred symbols, we enhance the potency of our intentions and align ourselves more deeply with the divine energies they represent.

Yantras: Sacred Geometric Diagrams

Yantras are intricate geometric diagrams that serve as visual representations of spiritual energies. They combine sacred geometry, symbolism, and mantra vibrations to create powerful tools for meditation and manifestation. Here's what you need to know about yantras:

Geometry and Proportions: Yantras are constructed using precise geometric shapes and proportions. These shapes, such as triangles, circles, and lotus petals, are carefully arranged to create intricate patterns that mirror the divine order of the universe. Each shape and pattern carries specific energetic qualities and represents different aspects of the divine.

Mantra Integration: Yantras are often inscribed with mantras or sacred syllables, including the Maha Mrityunjaya Mantra. The combination of the visual representation and the vibrational qualities of the mantra amplifies the yantra's power and facilitates a deeper connection with the divine energies it embodies.

Focus and Contemplation: Yantras are used as focal points for meditation and contemplation. By gazing upon the yantra, we direct our attention to its intricate details, allowing the mind to enter a state of focused concentration. This focused concentration opens the gateway to higher states of consciousness and facilitates a direct experience of the divine energies represented by the yantra.

Applying Sacred Symbols and Yantras

Here are some practical ways to apply sacred symbols and yantras in your spiritual practice and daily life:

Meditation and Contemplation: Incorporate yantra meditation into your daily practice. Choose a yantra that resonates with you and place it in your meditation space. Gaze upon the yantra with a relaxed yet focused gaze, allowing its geometric patterns to draw you into a state of inner stillness and expanded awareness.

Altar and Sacred Spaces: Create an altar or sacred space dedicated to the Maha Mrityunjaya Mantra and its associated symbols. Arrange yantras, along with other sacred objects and images, in a meaningful and harmonious way. This space will serve as a focal point for your spiritual practice and a reminder of the divine energies you are invoking.

Personal Empowerment: Wear or carry symbols that hold personal significance and represent your spiritual aspirations. This can be a pendant, a piece of jewellery, or a small symbol kept in your pocket or bag. These personal symbols act as reminders of your spiritual journey and intentions, keeping you connected to the divine energies throughout the day.

Rituals and Ceremonies: Incorporate sacred symbols and yantras into rituals and ceremonies. Use them as focal points for intention-setting, prayer, and invocation of specific energies. The presence of these symbols enhances the sacredness of the ritual and deepens your connection with the divine.

Manifestation and Intention Setting: Use yantras as tools for manifestation and intention setting. Choose a yantra that aligns with your specific intentions and place it in a prominent location in your home or workspace. Regularly gaze upon the yantra, infusing it with your intentions and allowing it to amplify your manifestation efforts.

Respect and Reverence

When working with sacred symbols and yantras, it is essential to approach them with respect and reverence. These symbols carry potent energies and are deeply intertwined with spiritual traditions and teachings. Here are some guiding principles:

Sacred Space: Create a sacred and clean space when working with sacred symbols and yantras. This space should be free from clutter and distractions, allowing you to fully engage with the energies they embody.

Pure Intentions: Approach the symbols and yantras with pure intentions, seeking spiritual growth, connection, and alignment with divine energies. Set aside egoistic desires and approach the symbols with humility and openness.

Proper Usage: Follow traditional guidelines and instructions for the usage and handling of sacred symbols and yantras. Respect cultural practices and protocols associated with these symbols, honouring the traditions from which they arise.

Energetic Cleansing: Regularly cleanse and purify your sacred symbols and yantras. This can be done through incense, sacred smoke, or intention-based rituals. Cleansing removes any stagnant or negative energies, ensuring the symbols retain their vibrancy and effectiveness.

By incorporating sacred symbols and yantras into your spiritual practice, you amplify the divine energies invoked through the Maha Mrityunjaya Mantra and deepen your connection with higher realms of consciousness.

Approach these symbols with respect, engage with them in meditation and contemplation, and allow their transformative power to guide you on your spiritual journey.

Chapter 13
Mystical Experiences and Realizations

In this chapter, we delve into the realm of mystical experiences and realizations that can arise through the practice of the Maha Mrityunjaya Mantra. As we engage with this sacred mantra, we open ourselves to profound spiritual insights, transformative shifts in consciousness, and direct experiences of the divine.

These mystical experiences and realizations have the power to awaken us to our true nature and deepen our connection with the eternal.

The Call of the Mystical

Throughout history, mystics, sages, and spiritual seekers have been drawn to the mystical path - a journey that transcends the boundaries of the ordinary and connects us with the infinite. The Maha Mrityunjaya Mantra serves as a potent catalyst for mystical experiences, inviting us to explore the depths of our being and encounter the divine within. Here are some aspects of the mystical journey:

Transcending the Ego: Mystical experiences often involve a temporary dissolution of the ego, allowing us to transcend our limited sense of self and merge with a greater, interconnected reality. In this state, we experience a profound sense of unity and oneness with all creation.

Expanded Consciousness: Mystical experiences expand our consciousness beyond the ordinary realms of perception. We may access heightened states of awareness, transcendent visions, or direct experiences of divine presence. These experiences can profoundly shift our understanding of reality and our place within it.

Non-Dual Awareness: Mystical realizations often point to the underlying non-dual nature of existence. We recognize the illusion of separation and the interconnectedness of all things. This realization opens the door to a deeper understanding of the fundamental unity that permeates all aspects of life.

Awakening to the Eternal

The practice of the Maha Mrityunjaya Mantra can act as a powerful catalyst for awakening to the eternal nature of our being. As we engage with the mantra's vibrations, we begin to peel away the layers of conditioning and limited perception, revealing the timeless essence that resides within. Here are some aspects of this awakening:

Direct Experience of the Divine: Through the Maha Mrityunjaya Mantra, we can experience direct communion with the divine. This may take the form of a deep sense of connection, a profound inner knowing, or a palpable presence that transcends the boundaries of the physical world. These experiences awaken us to the inherent divinity within and expand our understanding of the sacred.

Dissolving Illusions: The practice of the mantra has the potential to dissolve illusions and reveal the truth of our existence. We may come to recognize the impermanence of the physical realm and the eternal nature of our soul. This realization liberates us from the fear of death and empowers us to embrace life with greater courage and authenticity.

Remembering Our True Nature: The Maha Mrityunjaya Mantra acts as a reminder of our true nature as immortal beings. As we chant or meditate upon the mantra, we align ourselves with the vibrations of immortality and reawaken our innate wisdom and divine potential.

Integration and Embodiment

Mystical experiences and realizations are not meant to be fleeting moments but catalysts for transformation and integration into our daily lives. Here are some ways to integrate and embody the mystical insights gained through the Maha Mrityunjaya Mantra:

Integration through Contemplation: Set aside time for contemplation and reflection after engaging with the mantra. Journal your experiences, insights, and realizations, allowing them to deepen and integrate into your conscious awareness. Contemplate the significance of these experiences and explore how they can inform your actions and choices.

Living with Presence: Bring the essence of your mystical experiences into your everyday life by cultivating presence and mindfulness. Engage fully in each moment, recognizing the inherent divinity in all beings and the interconnectedness of all things. Embrace the eternal within the ordinary.

Service and Compassion: Let your mystical realizations inspire acts of service and compassion. Recognize the divine spark in others and extend love, kindness, and understanding. By living in alignment with the wisdom gained through mystical experiences, you become a vehicle for positive transformation in the world.

Continual Practice: Embrace the Maha Mrityunjaya Mantra as a lifelong practice. Engage with it regularly, allowing it to deepen your connection with the mystical realms and nourish your spiritual growth. Cultivate a sense of curiosity and openness, remaining receptive to new insights and experiences that arise along the journey.

Mystical experiences and realizations are profound gifts on the spiritual path, offering glimpses into the infinite and awakening us to our true nature. Through the practice of the Maha Mrityunjaya Mantra, we can open ourselves to these transformative experiences, allowing them to guide us towards greater understanding, unity, and divine communion.

Chapter 14
Connecting with the Divine: Rituals and Offerings

In this chapter, we explore the significance of rituals and offerings as a means of connecting with the divine through the practice of the Maha Mrityunjaya Mantra. Rituals and offerings have been an integral part of spiritual traditions across cultures and have served as powerful tools for deepening our relationship with the divine.

By understanding the purpose and symbolism behind these practices, we can enhance our spiritual journey and foster a deeper connection with the sacred.

The Power of Rituals

Rituals are symbolic actions performed with intention and reverence, designed to create a sacred space and establish a connection with the divine. They serve as bridges between the physical and spiritual realms, allowing us to engage with the deeper dimensions of existence. Here are some key aspects of rituals:

Creating Sacred Space: Rituals help create a sacred space that is conducive to spiritual practice. Whether it is through the arrangement of sacred objects, the lighting of candles, or the chanting of mantras, rituals create an environment that supports our connection with the divine.

Setting Intentions: Rituals provide a structured way to set intentions and focus our attention on specific spiritual goals. By clarifying our intentions before engaging in a ritual, we align ourselves with the energy and purpose of the practice, amplifying its impact on our consciousness.

Ritual as Remembrance: Rituals often involve the repetition of sacred actions and chants, serving as a way to remember and honour spiritual teachings and traditions. Through the repetition of rituals, we reinforce our commitment to the path and invoke the presence of the divine in our lives.

Offerings as Sacred Exchange

Offerings play a significant role in spiritual practices, serving as acts of devotion, gratitude, and surrender. They are a way of engaging in a sacred exchange with the divine, recognizing the abundance and blessings that flow into our lives. Here are some aspects of offerings:

Symbolic Gestures: Offerings can take various forms, such as flowers, incense, food, or sacred objects. These offerings hold symbolic significance and are meant to convey our reverence and gratitude towards the divine. Each offering carries a unique vibration and intention, establishing a sacred connection with the divine.

Cultivating Gratitude: Offerings provide an opportunity to cultivate a deep sense of gratitude for the blessings in our lives. As we make offerings, we acknowledge and express appreciation for the abundance and grace that surrounds us. This practice of gratitude opens our hearts and strengthens our connection with the divine.

Surrender and Detachment: Through offerings, we practice surrendering the fruits of our actions to the divine. It is a reminder that our actions are not driven by personal desires but are offered selflessly for the highest good. This act of surrender helps cultivate detachment and reduces our attachment to the outcomes of our endeavours.

Personalizing Your Rituals and Offerings

While rituals and offerings hold deep-rooted traditions and symbolism, it is essential to personalize them to align with our individual spiritual journey. Here are some suggestions to personalize your rituals and offerings:

Intention and Meaning: Reflect on the intentions and meaning behind the rituals and offerings. Consider the specific aspects of the divine that resonate with you and incorporate symbols or objects that hold personal significance.

Creative Expression: Explore creative ways to express your devotion and connection with the divine. You can create artwork, write poetry, or engage in activities that evoke a sense of reverence and connection. Let your heart guide you in finding unique expressions of devotion.

Mindful Presence: Approach your rituals and offerings with mindfulness and presence. Engage in them wholeheartedly, allowing yourself to be fully present in each action. Cultivate an attitude of reverence and surrender as you connect with the divine.

Rituals of Service: Consider how you can incorporate acts of service as offerings. Engage in selfless acts of kindness and compassion, dedicating the positive energy generated to the well-being of others and the world.

By personalizing your rituals and offerings, you infuse them with your unique energy and intention, deepening your connection with the divine. Remember, the essence of rituals and offerings lies not in the external form, but in the sincerity of your heart and the depth of your devotion.

Chapter 15
Living as an Immortal: Embracing the Eternal Essence

In this final chapter of our journey with the Maha Mrityunjaya Mantra, we delve into the profound wisdom and practical guidance for living as an immortal being. The practice of this mantra has the power to awaken us to our true nature and transform our perception of ourselves and the world around us.

By embracing the eternal essence within, we can live a life imbued with purpose, joy, and limitless possibilities.

Awakening to Immortality

The Maha Mrityunjaya Mantra serves as a catalyst for awakening us to the eternal essence that resides within each of us. It is a reminder that our true nature is beyond the transient nature of the physical body and the fluctuations of the mind. Here are key aspects of living as an immortal being:

Transcending the Fear of Death: Immortality does not imply physical immortality, but rather a realization that our essence transcends the limitations of the mortal body. By cultivating a deep understanding of our true nature, we can transcend the fear of death and embrace the impermanence of life as an opportunity for growth, transformation, and self-realization.

Connecting with the Source: Living as an immortal being involves recognizing our innate connection with the divine source from which all life emanates. We cultivate a conscious relationship with this source, whether we call it God, the Universe, or by any other name, and align our thoughts, actions, and intentions with its divine wisdom and guidance.

Embracing the Eternal Now: Immortality exists in the present moment. By anchoring ourselves in the eternal now, we release attachment to the past and the anxieties of the future. We fully embrace the richness and potential of each moment, knowing that it is an opportunity for spiritual growth and self-realization.

Living with Purpose and Authenticity

As immortal beings, we are called to live a life of purpose and authenticity, aligned with our deepest values and aspirations. Here are key aspects of living as an immortal being:

Discovering Your Soul's Purpose: Immortality invites us to explore our soul's purpose and align our lives with it. By connecting with our inner wisdom and listening to the whispers of our soul, we can uncover our unique gifts, passions, and contributions to the world. Living in alignment with our purpose brings fulfilment and meaning to our existence.

Cultivating Authenticity: Authenticity is the essence of living as an immortal being. By embracing our true selves, we let go of masks, pretences, and societal expectations. We honour our values, embrace our strengths and vulnerabilities, and express ourselves authentically in all aspects of life. Authentic living allows us to connect deeply with others and create meaningful relationships.

Embracing Limitless Possibilities: Living as an immortal being opens us to a realm of infinite possibilities. We release self-imposed limitations and expand our vision of what is possible in our lives. We tap into our creative potential, embrace curiosity and openness, and fearlessly pursue our dreams and aspirations.

Nurturing Spiritual Practices

To support our journey as immortal beings, it is essential to nurture our spiritual practices. These practices provide the foundation for our growth, self-realization, and connection with the divine. Here are key aspects of nurturing spiritual practices:

Sustaining the Maha Mrityunjaya Mantra Practice: The Maha Mrityunjaya Mantra continues to be a powerful tool for our spiritual journey. Regularly engage in the chanting or meditation on this mantra, allowing its sacred vibrations to deepen your connection with the eternal essence within.

Cultivating Mindfulness and Presence: Incorporate mindfulness and presence into your daily life. Be fully present in each moment, whether it is during mundane tasks or moments of joy and celebration. Cultivate awareness of your thoughts, emotions, and sensations, allowing yourself to experience the richness of life fully.

Seek Spiritual Guidance: Surround yourself with spiritual guidance and community. Seek the wisdom of teachers, mentors, or spiritual communities that resonate with your path. Engage in conversations, workshops, or retreats that nourish your spiritual growth and provide support along the journey.

Living in Unity and Love

Living as an immortal being involves recognizing the inherent unity and interconnectedness of all beings. It is through love and compassion that we transcend boundaries and embrace the oneness of existence. Here are key aspects of living in unity and love:

Cultivating Compassion: Cultivate compassion for all beings, recognizing the divine spark that resides within each individual. Practice kindness, empathy, and understanding, extending love and support to others on their own spiritual journeys.

Embracing Interconnectedness: Develop an awareness of the interconnectedness of all things. Recognize that our thoughts, words, and actions have a ripple effect on the world around us. Embrace a sense of responsibility for the well-being of the planet and its inhabitants, making choices that contribute to the greater good.

Radiating Love: Allow love to be the guiding force in your interactions and relationships. Radiate love unconditionally, embracing the power of love to heal, transform, and uplift. Through love, we transcend boundaries and create a harmonious and compassionate world.

Living as an immortal being is a lifelong journey of self-discovery, self-transcendence, and spiritual growth. It is an invitation to embrace the eternal essence within and live a life of purpose, authenticity, and love.

May the wisdom and practice of the Maha Mrityunjaya Mantra continue to guide you on this extraordinary journey of awakening to your immortal self.

As we conclude this book, let us remember that the journey towards immortality is not one of escaping the world but of fully embracing it with love, wisdom, and grace.

May you walk the path of the immortal with joy, inspiration, and reverence for the sacredness of life.

Conclusion

Congratulations! You have reached the end of our transformative journey through the pages of "Maha Mrityunjaya Mantra: Awaken the Immortal Within with Sacred Vibration Frequencies." We embarked on a profound exploration of the Maha Mrityunjaya Mantra and its potential to awaken the eternal essence within us.

Throughout this book, we delved into the meaning, significance, and practice of this sacred mantra, discovering its power to connect us with the divine and unleash our true potential.

As we come to the conclusion of this book, I invite you to reflect on the insights and practices shared within these pages. Take a moment to integrate the wisdom and teachings into your daily life, allowing them to permeate your being and guide your spiritual journey. Embrace the practice of the Maha Mrityunjaya Mantra as a sacred tool for self-discovery, transformation, and connection with the divine.

Remember that the journey of awakening to the immortal within is a lifelong pursuit. It requires dedication, patience, and an open heart. Each moment is an opportunity for growth and self-realization, and the Maha Mrityunjaya Mantra serves as a constant companion, supporting you in your quest for truth and liberation.

I would be immensely grateful if you could take a few moments to share your thoughts and feedback on this book. Your reviews are invaluable in helping others discover the transformative power of the Maha Mrityunjaya Mantra and its ability to awaken the immortal within. Your words have the potential to inspire and guide fellow seekers on their spiritual paths.

I would also encourage you to continue exploring the depths of the Maha Mrityunjaya Mantra. Dive deeper into the practices, meditations, and rituals shared in this book. Seek out additional resources, connect with like-minded individuals, and engage in further studies that resonate with your spiritual aspirations.

Remember, you are the embodiment of the immortal essence, connected to the divine source that flows through all of creation. Embrace the journey, honour your inner light, and radiate the wisdom and love that emanate from the depths of your being.

Thank you for joining me on this extraordinary voyage of self-discovery and awakening. May the Maha Mrityunjaya Mantra continue to guide you on your path, illuminating your way with its sacred vibrations and unlocking the limitless potential within you.

With deep gratitude and blessings,

Dr. Jilesh